The Hesitant Mistress

A Guide to Claiming Your Feminine Power

D. Hightower

Dyanna Hightower

ONEHAND PRESS

The Hesitant Mistress. © 2013 by Dvanna "Dawn" Hightower. All rights reserved.

Cover design by Dvanna Hightower
"A View from the Bottom" by Property

Library of Congress Cataloging-in-Publication Data
Hightower, Dvanna D.
   The Hesitant Mistress : A Guide to Claiming Your Feminine Power / Dvanna Hightower
ISBN-13: 978-1490379586
Self-Help / Sexual Instruction

Published internationally
OneHand Press, United States of America

The Hesitant Mistress

A Guide to Claiming Your Feminine Power

~ Contents ~

Preface

   A Warning for the Man in Her Life...........................1

Introduction

   Some Reassurances for the Hesitant Mistress...........5
   Your Journey...7
   The Dominant Female....................................8
   The Female-Led Relationship............................10
   Is This Abuse?...12
   The Submissive Male...................................14
   How It Works: A Brief Demonstration....................17

Gaining Confidence

   Being Yourself...23
   You are Attractive...24
   Stop Apologizing...26
   Say What You Mean..................................28
   Don't Justify..30
   Give Up Validation.....................................32
   Be Aware of Your Space..33
   Wear Something Sexy................................34
   Know You Can Handle It...35
   Become Self-Reliant.................................36
   Declare A Preference...............................37
   Lead, Don't Follow..................................39
   Vocalize Your Instincts...............................40

Training Him

You Were Made for This..45
Set Boundaries..46
Be Consistent..48
Set Expectations...50
Being Bossy...52
  Giving Orders..54
  Reward and Punish...57
Answers and Objections...62
It's Your Decision...64

Scening

Of Scenes and Bedrooms...71
Games to Start Out With..75
Safewords..77
Stop and Think About It..78
Take Your Time..79
Caring Too Much...81
Fetishes..83
Putting It All Into Practice..86
New Beginnings...88

Appendix

A View From the Bottom:
    A Submissive's Addendum..................................91
About the Author..95

*To women everywhere...
and to the hesitant mistress
I once knew so well.*

~ A Warning ~
For the Man in Her Life

THIS book will teach your partner how to be more dominant. That means she will learn how to actually be more dominant, not just how to act like a dominatrix long enough for you to get your jollies off in the bedroom.

Your partner will learn how to say no to you. She will learn how to train you. She will learn how to punish you and hold you accountable for your actions. She will learn that she can demand whatever she wants from you, despite whatever you might want from her.

So beware, my unsuspecting male friend... if you bought this book for her, you might get more than you asked for. You may want to quietly set it aside and buy her a set of fuzzy handcuffs instead.

You have been warned.

Part I

Introduction

~ Some Reassurances ~
For the Hesitant Mistress

Most likely, you've picked up this book in response to a conversation with the man in your life – your husband, your boyfriend, or someone you care about. If this is the case, congratulations, my dear reader. You are one lucky lady.

Being given this book means that your partner loves you enough to want to involve you in one of his deepest, most personal fantasies. He trusts you enough to admit his most vulnerable needs to you. And he is ready to pamper you in the most romantic, doting ways you've ever longed for from a partner... as soon as you tell him what they are.

This book may not yet seem like the blessing it is. Your partner's interests may baffle you. They may sound like an obligation to become someone you're not – someone cruel or bossy or sexually wild. But honoring your natural instincts is what this book is all about.

You aren't expected to put on an awkward show of being a dominatrix, complete with catsuit and whip. You won't need to "fake it till you make it." You are already your partner's mistress. Since the first day he met you, you have been the reigning force in his heart. The instant he confided his secret desires to you, he offered you the key to his soul. It's an act of romance touching beyond words.

By exploring the concepts in this book, you can learn to love and trust your partner even more deeply. You won't be required to hurt him or hurl insults at him. You aren't expected to be arrogant or spiteful. You can do whatever you want, at whatever pace you are comfortable with. It's a license to be yourself.

You've been given a magic lamp. Your secret wishes are yours for the asking. What would you like from your partner? If you want an extra round of sensual foreplay, it's yours; if you want a cozy date night without sex, just say so. What woman wouldn't like this arrangement?

By offering you this book, your partner hopes to show you the alluring potential of your inner power. You can choose to work with his tastes in fantasy, or not. That's the beauty of domination: you decide what is right for you. Stay true to yourself, honor your feelings, and you can never go wrong.

~ Your Journey ~

THIS book is divided into four sections.

The *Introduction,* which you are reading now, explains more about what it means to be a female dominant with a male submissive. (It's not as strange as you might think!)

The second section, *Gaining Confidence,* is about raising your self-esteem and assertiveness in everyday situations. You may grow from shy mouse to human being. (There's no need to become a roaring lion.)

The third section, *Training Him,* teaches you how to develop more discipline in your man. With your help, he will wash the dishes regularly like he's always promised to. (And he'll be happy to do it for you!)

The fourth section, *Scening,* is about fun experiments you can do in the bedroom. It is a no-obligation menu of sexy treats you might want to try out with your man. (No whip necessary.)

Whatever you think of this book, I can guarantee that it will help you look at your life in a whole new way. Enjoy the possibilities, and have fun!

~ THE DOMINANT FEMALE ~

MEN find confidence sexy. Like bright plumage on a bird, it sends out a mating signal of healthy vitality. When a woman holds her own, she sends up a shining flare of attraction from a sea of passive mediocrity.

It's interesting that this quality is so rare – that despite its obvious appeal, female confidence gets discouraged, maligned, and tamped down. Women are afraid to be self-assured, because it would be socially unacceptable for them to be too brash, bitchy, arrogant, or aggressive.

But there's a vast gulf between "timid" and "arrogant." Most women have settled for a mouselike existence of self-consciously hoping that everyone likes them. This is so ubiquitous as to be considered normal – when what *should* be normal would be holding a healthy, comfortable self-image.

This book will teach you to embrace your inner confidence, a self-image more concerned with real courage and integrity than with what others might think.

This book will not teach you to become the stereotypical dominatrix, a self-absorbed, overbearing psychopath. I know you don't want to become her. I'm sure your partner will agree.

What your partner *does* want is a woman who has her head on straight. She has opinions she believes in. She honors her feelings. She won't roll over at the first sign of resistance. Instead of saying "I dunno, what do *you* want to do tonight?" she suggests, "Let's stay in." (Mmm!) She knows where she wants to go and how to get there... so of course her smitten man will be happy to follow her lead.

That woman, my friend, is you.

~ The Female-Led Relationship ~

At first glance, our society seems patriarchal. The man in a marriage is said to be the provider, the protector, the decision-maker. He's supposed to pay the bills and make sure things get done.

Of course, anyone who has actually been married knows that life no longer works the same way it did for the ancient Greeks. Today, it's usually the woman who is the real head of the household. She manages all of the paperwork, planning, and "honey-do" lists. Her husband respects her opinion and asks for her permission on major purchases. And of course, if the wife isn't happy, the husband isn't going to be happy, either.

The female-led relationship simply acknowledges these facts aloud.

In a female-led relationship, there is no silly dance of catty manipulation and macho reluctance leading to misunderstandings and tearful arguments. The man admits that the woman's needs are just as valid as his. He knows that his happiness is dependent on hers. He remembers that his wife is not a trophy gathering dust on his mantelpiece; he is still her suitor, and her heart still deserves to be courted and won.

The man agrees to comply with his partner's wishes, whatever they may be, because he loves her and trusts her judgment. He understands that when she has a request, it's for a good reason, and he should honor it.

The woman in authority doesn't consider herself "better" than the man, any more than a coach considers himself better than his players. They are part of the same team.

In every relationship, a woman wants stability, respect, and love. What a submissive man wants is to give her that. These needs are symbiotically beneficial. When the dominant woman guides the submissive man, both partners' lives improve. You will gain a more pleasing partner and experience all of his heartfelt offerings of love. He, in turn, will enjoy your praise and your pleasure.

You know better than anyone else what you want from a man, and your partner wants to be the best man he can be for you. He has failed so many times at guessing what women want, it is a relief for him to hear what specific behavior you'd like to see from him. When he does well, he feels an almost spiritual joy from seeing you smile.

This is not a relationship run by an overbearing bully. The female dominant is a considerate lover who enters a willing partnership of mutual benefit.

No cruelty necessary.

~ Is This Abuse? ~

But what about this master and slave thing? What about whips and chains? What about spanking and scolding?

Since every mainstream depiction of female domination seems to involve the pain, humiliation, and scorn of men, it's no surprise that any sane woman would be reluctant to adopt this role in her relationship. If you love your man and want him to be happy, how can you treat him as if you hate him?

First, you must realize that most of what you've seen is exaggerated. It's pornography. You know, "Did you order a pizza, lady?" cheesy, goofy pornography. The actress's plumage is fanning out grandiose mating signals, drawing in customers. Guys can marvel at how this woman is *so* confident, she doesn't care what anyone else thinks. She will do whatever crazy thing she pleases to enjoy herself, even at the expense of others!

In real life, if you want to enjoy yourself, you might not do anything more abusive to your partner than ask him to run you a bubble bath. (So shocking!) Who can say? You won't know until you try.

Second, remember that yours is a partnership of two mutually consenting adults. Even with all of these seemingly abusive bedroom props like whips and chains, anything you decide to do to your self-appointed "slave" can only happen with his co-operation. You can (and should) discuss what he does and doesn't want to do, and have regular chats about what works for you both and what doesn't.

Oddly, even though it looks like the male in a female dominated relationship is forced to do things against his will, he has the option to back out at any time. He has the right to say "no." He just wants to test out the *illusion* of having no say. He thinks he'll like it, so he's asking for your help. If he doesn't like it, he can always ask you to stop. No harm done!

~ The Submissive Male ~

What sort of man comes to mind when you hear the words "submissive male?" It's probably someone pretty pathetic – a cowering weakling. He's a pansy, a pushover. He's the simpering wimp who fetches the coffee for the alpha male leading the boardroom.

But none of the submissive men I've met have fit this stereotype. They are virtually indistinguishable from the men around them. Often, the submissive male is the leader sitting at the head of that boardroom table. If there is one thing a submissive male is good at, it's pushing himself to perform.

The submissive man is not weak, any more than an obedient soldier or star athlete is weak. He will push himself hard to meet expectations. A structured environment helps him focus. If an authority points him in a direction and sets a deadline, he suddenly has a defined challenge to conquer.

He wants to be the best man he can be, and that means overcoming his faults. He hates that he cuts corners and procrastinates. He craves correction, even as he hates needing it. He doesn't want to slack off when no one's looking. He wants your high standards, your tough love. He wants you to accept nothing less than his best effort.

The submissive man will accept guidance only if he knows it's good for him. He is not a doormat, someone too helpless to protest as others walk all over him. He has the right to complain, to question, to call a halt to any situation he disagrees with. Submission is an escape from the ordinary, not a personality trait.

That said, there does appear to be some inborn attraction to submission; some brains seem wired for it. Typically, the submissive male will experience an endorphin rush when he obeys an order. He feels a thrill when he overcomes his own selfish impulses.

You see, the submissive male does not automatically do whatever you say. Just like everyone else, he feels a momentary resistance to being told what to do. But he purposely presses through this. Like a high diver swallowing his fear, the submissive swallows his pride. His spiritual leap into surrender is not a show of weakness. It takes great strength.

The skills developed through submission are considered virtues in many religions – humility, service, and valor. It takes an admirable amount of maturity to acquiesce to someone's better judgment. It takes courage to trust their guidance. It takes fortitude to complete the assigned task – especially if that task is painful or humbling.

It takes an incredible amount of bravery to even admit to having these desires. Every young boy is taught that he should always fight to be top dog. He learns that it's especially humiliating to be beaten by a girl. He worries that respecting women will make him less of a man, when really, it makes him more of one – a particularly brave and romantic man.

Far from being a pathetic wimp, this boy grows up to be a man most women would consider the ideal mate. He opens doors. He helps with the chores. He is attentive in bed. He puts his lover on a pedestal. His greatest goal in life is to make her smile. There is romance in his soul – a deep and burning desire to give everything he is for her.

Like all men, the submissive male wants to be a hero.

He will strive to be a knight for his lady – walking through fire for her, slaying her dragons, and fighting to earn her favor. He will endure pain, toil, indignity, and bondage to prove himself to her. He will guard and defend her with his life.

The submissive knight trusts his queen enough to relax his guard in front of her. He is brave enough to let her see the darkest parts of himself so she can set him back on the right path.

Why does he need to do all of this? Why does he like the thought of sacrificing himself? Why does he want to give up so much control?

The answers to these questions are as varied as the men. Submissive men come from all walks of life and find different things alluring. There is nothing wrong with any of them, any more than there is something wrong with you for reading the occasional erotic novel. Ideas can be sexy. They can be enthralling. They can haunt your sexual fantasies for a lifetime... until one day, you work up the courage to admit them to your partner.

So talk to your partner. Be curious. Ask questions, be understanding, and he will confide his most amazing secret hopes to you.

It's okay if you're hesitant to jump in and try out every idea your partner brings up. Just listen to him. Be patient. Be compassionate. Chances are, he is both embarrassed about his fantasies and hopeful you'll find them as exciting as he does. Even if you don't understand all of his motivations, he needs you to reassure him that you still love him no matter what.

Be gentle with him, for he is giving you the gift of his heart. He hopes you will grant him this chance to prove himself to you.

~ How It Works ~
A Brief Demonstration

An average day in a female-led relationship is a seamless flow of giving and receiving. The dominant/submissive arrangement helps the couple provide each other with what they want. Their needs complement each other.

In my relationship, I love pampering. My partner loves doting on me. I have learned to use my confidence to train him to fawn over me in the ways I prefer, which we both find alluring enough to take into the bedroom at night.

You will learn all of these skills as you progress through the book and work with your partner. Your relationship may end up looking different than mine, because your desires will be different. For now, take a peek at my morning and imagine your own possibilities....

My day begins in the arms of my man, cuddled up in bed. We nuzzle each other until my need to get up trumps my need to fondle him. Then I poke him in the chest and say, "Go make coffee."

He wallows for a second, reluctant to leave my embrace. Then he rolls out of bed and trots off to the kitchen. He knows I won't let him laze around when he has a job to do.

Minutes later, I'm dressed and sitting down at the computer. My lover bows, offering me a cappuccino.

"Do it right," I say.

He drops to his knees, raising his arms in just the way I've taught him, and formally presents the mug to me.

"Better," I allow, giving him a pat. I take the coffee from his hands. It's creamy and decadent, made just the way I like it.

"May I have a cup of coffee?" he asks.

"Yes," I answer politely. I rarely say "no" to these requests. I just appreciate that he asks permission, and he knows that.

He sits at his own computer, sipping coffee and waking up for a while. Then he gets up, slipping into the adjacent kitchen to make breakfast.

My phone dings; he has sent me an email. Every morning, he completes an assignment to inform me of his schedule for the day. I have requested this routine because it helps me make my own plans.

I look over his list. "You have a client at 2, and grocery shopping at 6? I thought I told you to go grocery shopping yesterday."

"Yes, Ma'am," he replies. "But there was that problem with the car..."

"Oh, that's right."

"I'm sorry, Ma'am. I should have walked to the nearest store before bed. Do you want me to get the paddle?"

"No, dear. I understand. You had a lot to deal with yesterday."

"Yes, Ma'am. Thank you for understanding, Ma'am."

Soon, he brings me an amazing home-cooked breakfast: eggs, bacon, a muffin. I know he would cook almost the same thing for himself if he were alone, but when he makes it for me, it adds a special sweetness to this part of his routine. And when I'm there, he gets to add thoughtful touches, like the butter and honey I like. It warms my heart.

"May I sit at the table with you?" he asks, holding his own plate.

"No, sit at my feet." This little gesture of dominance – simply putting him in a spot lower than mine – comforts him, reminding him of his place. It's what he signed up for, after all.

"Yes, Ma'am." He settles down next to me, content.

"This is very good," I compliment him. "Thank you, boy. I love your cooking."

"My pleasure, Ma'am."

I prop my feet in his lap. He kisses my leg tenderly, and we share a few minutes of peace while we eat.

Sometimes, when we give and take orders like this, the silence is loaded with sexual tension. Today, it's just companionable affection. We love being near each other, balancing our desires off each other.

At last, I hand him my dish, and he clears the table. There are a few crumbs left on my plate, which he will personally clean off. He likes the idea of eating my scraps; I like how eagerly he washes the dishes.

"Anything else, Ma'am?"

"No, go get ready for work. Wear your collar under your shirt. I'll be chaining it to the bed when you get home."

"Yes, Ma'am!"

"Oh, and put the paddle in the bedroom. I don't want to see a repeat of that lazy little bow you did when you presented my coffee this morning. I've trained you to assume specific positions for me. Let's see if you can remember them all, tonight."

Part II

Gaining Confidence

~ Being Yourself ~

If you're going to be asking your partner for favors, you need to at least feel worthy enough to accept those favors. If you have low self-esteem, making "selfish" requests may sound conceited and pushy.

But your partner already wants to assist you. It is rewarding for him, in much the same way you might love to give gifts to friends. He wants to demonstrate his love. All you need to do is feel comfortable accepting his attention.

You are valuable enough to deserve this. You matter. You don't have to shrink yourself into nothing for the sake of being "nice." You don't have to be invisible. You can learn to believe in yourself.

You might not be one of those women who ends every sentence with a question mark... but I once was. As I slowly graduated from mouse to human being, I got quite a few insights into how the average woman can beat herself down. In the next few chapters, I will offer you a hand up. Take your time and test out these concepts in day-to-day life. You'll learn to like who you see. You are wonderful, whether you believe it or not. (Your partner certainly thinks so!)

Confidence is already inside you, waiting to come out. It's behind that uneasy feeling of suppression; it's your natural competence, stopped and questioned.

Learn to trust yourself. You won't turn into a snarling dominatrix. You'll just turn into... you. And that makes it a lot easier to stand your ground.

~ You Are Attractive ~

Society has made women neurotic about how they look. We're bombarded with images telling us that our hair is not curly enough, straight enough, blond or red or dark or light enough. We're too short, too tall, not curvy enough, not thin enough, not the right color, and not the right age.

What is "enough?" What is the all-encompassing ideal we must reach, and what happens when we get there? Is it "when I don't want to change myself anymore?" (Good luck chasing that tail.) Is it "when men only look at me, and not at other women?" (Ha, ha!)

If you judge yourself by what you imagine men prefer, then you need a more freeing and realistic perspective. Men prefer you as you are. Really.

You have to realize, men think of women in the same way that women think of chocolate. Chocolate is always a good thing (always!), only regretfully ever turned down. It doesn't matter what's in the box assortment; every single flavor can be savored in different ways. There is no official winner. Sure, some men will prefer dark chocolate, and some men will prefer white chocolate, but neither one of those varieties is the ideal chocolate for men in general. There will always, always be a connoisseur out there looking for you – exactly you, exactly as you already are. He thinks you're perfect; you're his favorite flavor. You're already delicious, to him and to others.

It's hard to believe, so I suggest you register on a few online personals websites and see. Place a free ad for a week, just to sit back and watch the fish nibble. (This is a noncommittal experiment; stay anonymous and let your partner know you're not seriously looking.) Within minutes, the offers will start rolling in.

You will receive "spray and pray" emails addressed to Female, Any Female. There will be jerks who insult you, trying to "play" you into sleeping with them. And there will be dozens of good men sending hopeful inquiries because they honestly like you, and they would honestly like to get to know you. It's a tremendous ego boost.

Women can waste their lives in insecurity, trying to be perfect enough to win a man. It's a wake-up call to realize that the situation is exactly the opposite – that you are the prize the men have been trying to win. Men have an addiction to feed, a craving to fix, and *you* are the drug they desire. There's no way around it; they are powerless before your charms.

So men already love you. The question becomes, why not love yourself? Why bother with all of this stupid magazine-prescribed self-loathing? Why try to conform to a beauty ideal that doesn't actually exist and isn't even necessary for the mating process? Why consent to making yourself unhappy?

Be happy. Be content. Be yourself, and men will fall at your feet. It's what they do.

~ Stop Apologizing ~

Our society teaches women to apologize for existing. Have you noticed that it always seems to be a female who says "Excuse me," and scurries out of the way when two people bump into each other? Have you ever apologized for "being a bother" when you make a request? How many times have you seen a woman say "Sorry!" as she blots tears from her eyes?

That is not right. It is not healthy. A fully functional human being should be allowed to feel emotions. A normal member of society should be allowed to have needs. They should be able to take up space without feeling like they're standing in someone else's way. We are equal beings in an egalitarian culture, and it's time to act like it.

So stop pussyfooting around. Don't preface your statements with "I know I'm just being silly, but..." and "Correct me if I'm wrong." Don't add a disclaimer to your beliefs like "no offense," or "just my two cents." You have a point of view. Own it. Don't dismiss it even before anyone else can. If you don't think your own opinions count, no one else will, either. Take a stand and don't apologize for it.

Don't misunderstand my meaning, here. There is a time and place for apologies. A good dominant, male or female, will always admit when they are at fault. In cases where an apology is really warranted, being humble will earn you more respect, not less.

The next time you feel the urge to say you're sorry, ask yourself if you really are – or if you're just trying to make sure that somebody likes you. Suck it up, swallow that apology, and see what it feels like to be disliked. Truth is, the person you're talking to probably won't even notice how terrible you are. You'll just sound like a human being with the same worth and value as everyone else.

And eventually you'll realize that you should listen to your own opinions. They have a lot to say.

~ Say What You Mean ~

GROWING up, little girls learn to be cute to get what they want. They giggle, they flutter their eyelids, and they act helpless. If they say "gimme!" they are told it's not polite. As these girls get older, they learn to behave nicely even when angry; they are reduced to acting out their needs through cattiness and passive aggression. Their poor boyfriends have to navigate a labyrinth of manipulative, pleasant-sounding code phrases that don't mean what they say, like "Nothing, I'm fine," and "Go ahead."

It's time we grew out of this.

Looking back through my first emails as a dominant, I shudder to read the hedging my male partner had to wade through. Instead of saying "Call me every morning with a status report," I would hint that "I'd like to hear from you more often, on a more regular basis.... I like to be kept up to date on what's going on in your life, you know."

In hindsight, I think my hesitancy came from a faint sense of fear. What if my partner thought my demands were too demanding? What if he questioned the need for them? What if he said no? If I wasn't explicit, then I couldn't be held accountable. I wouldn't have to explain myself – my feelings, my needs.

But, of course, vagueness is a recipe for disappointment. My partner never sent me answers to more than four out of five questions I'd buried in an email. He missed the hint that Thursday could be a special day. He didn't know that I like flowers more than chocolates.

Why? Because I didn't tell him.

Men are straightforward creatures. They need data, specifications, lists. If you say you want more help with the chores, prepare to be disappointed. If you say you want him to wash the sheets every Tuesday, his reaction will be much more gratifying.

If your man doesn't seem thoughtful enough for your tastes, you may not have identified your needs clearly enough for him. Sure, you want your partner to be more romantic – but what does that look like to you? Does it mean you want him to surprise you with funny gifts, cook you a candlelit dinner, greet you with a kiss, or rub your feet after a long day at the office? Are these behaviors required or optional? Do you have preferences on the details? Figure out what you want, then tell your partner. You can't expect him to guess what you like before you've even decided what it is. In order for him to fulfill your needs, he must hear what they are.

Also be aware that your partner can't keep track of everything you mention. Submissive men are not computers, and they forget things without meaning to. If something is important to you, demand it particularly – in a list, enforced with training. Highlight it for your partner, so he can highlight it for himself. He will do the best he can to follow your orders.

~ Don't Justify ~

"You know how some women get really upset when you leave the toilet seat up or you squeeze the toothpaste tube the wrong way? Well, I've never been that way. I was always pretty easygoing, and even my big brothers couldn't rile me up as a kid. So if I get upset over something, it's probably pretty important, and it means I have put a lot of thought into it. I've heard other people complain about this, too, so it's not so strange that I think it's upsetting. Anyway, there's some soap scum in the bathtub, and it's gotten so slippery I'm afraid I'm going to fall and hurt myself soon, and you wouldn't want to have to take me to the hospital, would you? So if you have the time and it's not too much bother, would you clean the tub? Look, I'm not criticizing you, and I know you have a lot to do, but it's not a very hard job, and it shouldn't take you too long. I remember you said you'd get to it last week, anyway, so you really should...."

If you got tired of sitting through this, just imagine how your partner would feel. If you want him to clean your bathtub, just say, "Clean the bathtub." Or maybe, "Clean the bathtub, please." That's all he needs. He doesn't need to hear all of the reasons you're asking him to do it. He doesn't want to hear how justified your request is. If you explain your reasoning, he will be mentally yawning and tuning out your nagging halfway through your speech. He can hardly say yes when you're listing all the reasons he might say no.

You're allowed to have a desire. Really. You don't have to prove that your desire is okay.

Your life is not a debate. Disagreement will not kill you. You don't have to forestall all possible objections in advance. If your partner has a concern, then you can talk it out as necessary. This is not hard to handle. It's how a normal conversation works.

Just give your man one sentence, the meat of the matter. Get to the point. Tell your partner what you want boldly and unapologetically, and let him decide what he thinks about it. He will appreciate it.

~ Give Up Validation ~

ASKING for validation is a bad habit, and it never actually works. Even if you believe what your man says about how nice your butt looks in that dress, you'll still be a black hole of insecurity the next time you put something on.

If you let others determine how you feel about things, you will never learn to trust your own feelings. And if you don't trust your own feelings, how can you learn to trust yourself?

Stop seeking consensus. Your common sense is working just fine. There's no need to look for moral support and verification on internet forums. No, you're not being unreasonable; yes, you should probably see another doctor; yes, you should dump a boyfriend who sneaks home smelling like perfume. If you already know the answer, why bother asking for advice? Do you really trust yourself so little that an anonymous second opinion will make you feel safer?

Why would you need to hear unanimous agreement from your girlfriends? As some sort of permission to feel the way you already feel? Why trust their half-informed guesses more than your own instincts?

Why follow the crowd? Carve your own path. Be your own leader. You just have to be brave enough to step out on your own.

No one else can reassure you. You can only reassure yourself. And soon enough, you won't even have to bother with assurance... because you'll trust yourself.

~ Be Aware of Your Space ~

Shy women shrink. They fold themselves into as small of a space as possible, against a wall, in a corner, hunched over, arms closed.

Confident women take up more space. They claim it. They own it. They have a broad stance. They rest their hands on their hips. They spread their arms along seat backs. They prop their feet up. They lounge. They gesture for others to sit around them.

On one memorable occasion, my partner exclaimed, "You are such a badass!" simply because I was sitting with one elbow cocked out.

Try it now. Change your resting posture, and see if it makes you feel more powerful. Then, get into the habit of relaxing that way.

Notice where you walk in public areas. Is it along the walls, or in the middle of the corridor? Do you step aside for others to pass, or do they defer to you? See if you can adopt a healthy, comfortable bubble of personal space. It's a nice thing to own.

~ Wear Something Sexy ~

PUT on your lacy panties and push-up bra. You know, the ones that make you feel too sexy for polite company. Style your hair. Curl your eyelashes. Cross your legs slowly and sensually. Tell the world that you feel like wearing heels to bed tonight, and you just need a man to hold open a door for you.

Play dress up. Play diva. Don't do it for them. Do it for you.

There's just something about looking fabulous that makes you feel fabulous. And when you feel fabulous every day, you come to accept that you *are* fabulous. Whether you are wearing sneakers or an evening gown, your man is lucky to have you in his life – and you're lucky enough to know it. (Most women never find out!)

~ Know You Can Handle It ~

You can handle anything. Fires, earthquakes, homelessness, bankruptcy, famine, plague, the zombie apocalypse. Refusal, rebuttal, rejection. Anything.

How do I know? Because you've handled everything so far.

I don't care what you've been through – illness, abuse, financial hardship – you came through it and survived. I know, my dear reader, because you're reading this right now.

Those things might have been terrifying at the time. You might have thought you were going to die. You might have felt despair beyond anything you've ever known. But you still made it through.

Confidence is knowing that you can survive anything that life throws at you. You can handle it. You may not handle it perfectly, but you will handle it perfectly well.

All you have to do is take things one step at a time... the same way you always have.

~ BECOME SELF-RELIANT ~

THERE is no problem you can't solve on your own. The trick is just not giving up too early.

So, the sink is making a funny noise. Is there some reason that your husband would be able to pinpoint the source of it any faster than you? Being male does not give him superior repairman powers. He will do exactly the same things as you – look down the drains, test the water, jiggle the connections. He will look it up on the internet. He will, if necessary, call a plumber. (Actually, you probably have him beat on that one.)

Why would your partner know where this street ends? Why would he have a better idea of what those strange guys down the road are doing? Why would he be able to tell you why your e-mail isn't working? He has no more answers than you do. He is just more used to being asked.

You are an adult, not a fairy tale princess. Be able to rescue yourself under your own power, whether it be from plumbing emergencies or bad life decisions. Retain access to your own keys, money, and phone so you can't be held hostage to someone else's idiocy. Have tools available to you so you can take that next step on your own.

The next time you run into some little obstacle and have the urge to ask for help… don't. You won't become an expert on saving yourself until you try. And there is nothing like the confidence you get from solving a problem on your own.

~ Declare a Preference ~

"Where do you want to eat?" your man asks.

"I don't care," you say. And you're doing yourself a disservice.

Maybe you think you don't have a preference, but you do. If you pay attention to your own internal state, you will feel a resistance to Chinese, an aversion to anything with shellfish in it, and a strange attraction to Italian meatballs. It's all right there in blazing emotional color. Listen to it. Air it. Set it free.

At other times, you won't have a preference at first. Maybe you don't have enough knowledge of the subject at hand. Maybe you need to know the movie times before you can pick which one you'd like to see. Maybe you need to find out which restaurant is closer to your office. Tell your partner. Even better, enlist his help in doing your research.

When all is said and done and you still don't have a clear preference… pick something anyway.

I know. It's scandalous. It's almost like you're lying. You're taking a stand while not totally sure of yourself. Realize this, honey: men do that twenty-four hours a day. They take risks; they bullshit. It's a function of testosterone. They aren't actually more certain than you are. They're just less careful. And really, isn't a careful leader much more qualified to lead?

So pick a path at that fork in the road. Declare your hidden preferences. This takes practice. You have to trust yourself enough to be selfish. This goes against everything we've been taught as women.

Being selfish sounds unfair. It sounds unequally weighted. It's not. Being *selfless* is unequally weighted. Being accommodating is unfair to you.

Having an opinion puts you on the same playing field as everyone else. It makes you as worthy of leadership as anyone else.

What does your leadership look like? Are you a spoiled tyrant pushing an agenda? Of course not! You're the same reasonable person you always were. If your partner has a differing opinion, you'll listen to it and take all possibilities into account. You'll favor the choice that makes the most sense for both of you. (Of course you will! Why wouldn't you?)

The only shocking new development, here, is that as the authority figure, you officially get the final say. And that's pretty nice.

Your partner doesn't think your opinions are selfish. He values your insight. He wants you to give him some guidance. Try it. You'll grow to like it.

~ Lead, Don't Follow ~

Don't allow yourself to be led around in a daze. Pay attention. Pick a table. Pick a seat for yourself and your friend. Know where the exits are. Have an idea of where you'd like to go next. Know if it is north or south of your location.

Have some foresight. If you're going out on a date, know which restaurant you'd like to eat at and which movie you'd like to see. Have an idea of who will be driving, what time you'd like to come home, and what you'd like to do once you get there.

Take responsibility for more decisions. If you're sitting in a bar and your partner isn't sure which drink he wants, make a choice for him. His day is full of these little uncertainties, and by taking charge, you can be a reassuring source of stability in his life. (Plus, he secretly finds it hot.)

~ Vocalize Your Instincts ~

THERE'S a little voice that pipes up inside you every time something is not right. Over the years you've been taught to stifle it, because it's not polite to say "excuse me?!" and "I won't put up with this crap from you." But no matter how much you squelch it, you know that voice is always right.

Notice the next time you get that uneasy sense of holding back. Notice how you tell yourself "It's not that important" or "I'll get over it in a minute." Then speak up: say "Hey…" and explain what you're feeling. "Hey, that tone of voice rubs me the wrong way." "Hey, I don't need your help." "Hey, who do you think is in charge here?" Just the simple act of saying "Hey" will break through that wall of hesitation and let your true feelings pour out.

Dominance isn't about being bossy, cruel, sexy, or anything else. It's about honoring that voice enough to share it out loud. Whether you're picking a restaurant or defending your honor, it's all the same voice: a trust in yourself.

When you are training a man, the voice will tell you when he's trying to cut corners, when he's testing you, and when he's ready to break. It will tell you what he needs to work on and what you should concentrate on next. It will tell you how far to push, where, and what will motivate him to try harder.

When my man picks up his cell phone to check his texts, that voice tells me to make him ask for permission. When he tries to hand me something instead of presenting it to me on his knees, the voice tells me to make him kneel and do it right.

That quiet inner voice is magical, really. If you listen to it, it will give you all that you wish for.

Part III

Training Him

~ You Were Made for This ~

LADIES everywhere want to change their man. You actually can. And it will be with his willing consent and cooperation.

Mothers nurture children, teaching them to grow up into responsible human beings. In a loving and compassionate way, they point out transgressions, praise good behavior, and use consequences to instill discipline. As a woman, you have an innate talent for this careful correction.

Your partner knows this, and he wants your guidance. He wants your tough love. He wants you to point out that he didn't wash the dishes like he said he would. He wants you to refuse to give in when he whines and gives excuses. He wants you to make him do it over again – and do it right, this time.

He knows these are his failures as a man. He wants to be the best man he can be for you. He wants you to be proud to call him yours. He wants to never disappoint you ever again. He wants to do whatever he can to make you happy. It's so sweet!

All you have to do to reap the rewards is tap into your natural instincts – that small voice mentioned in the last chapter. Listen deeply to this feminine intuition, and it will point the way.

~ Set Boundaries ~

In the same way that little kids will run out of sight until called back, men will test how much they can get away with. They are constantly looking to you for cues that will tell them how much you will allow. Will you let them get away with ogling other women? With not washing the dishes? With not offering to pay for dinner? Once allowed, your man will continue to do these things from now on.

Like children, submissive men need the security of knowing that someone cares enough to keep them safe from their mistakes. They find it reassuring to know the limits of their sandbox – what they need to do in class, and when recess is out. And they find a certain pleasurable tension in knowing that there's something out there they could possibly get away with. (Of course, they would never admit any of this.)

If your man's behavior bothers you in any way, you have the power to stop it. Just put your foot down. Say no. If he asks why, you can explain why it bothers you. But the important thing is to stand your ground.

Don't back down. His behavior is unacceptable, period. It doesn't matter that he was tired, or forgetful, or had extenuating circumstances; if he screws up, he deserves correction. And he knows it.

Consider all of the people in authority over you – the tax man, your boss, your dean. You can't argue with them. You can't wriggle your way out from under their expectations. You're stuck doing whatever they say. You might even have to thank them when you're done.

You are that authority figure. It doesn't matter what happened in the office today. You're still the boss. No amount of wheedling will invert your position over your employees. What you say goes.

Some women can't imagine having this much power in their relationship, because they imagine that authority is synonymous with physical size or standing armies. But you are already in charge. You're reading this book, your partner is a submissive male, and all the threat you need is already hanging over his head.

You see, your partner's fondest wish is to submit to you. If he undermines your authority, it means he undermines his own happiness. If he refuses to cooperate with your requests, you can simply stop playing his game. (After all, why would you bother giving orders to someone who won't obey them?)

His future depends upon satisfying you now. If he wants to be happy, he will have to keep you happy. One sharp look from you is all it takes to remind him of that.

~ Be Consistent ~

Rules are rules. It's meaningless to say "No swimming" one day and "Well, it's hot today, so I guess it's okay" the next. If you set a boundary for your man, be ready to enforce it consistently. If he learns that he can just wait until you are too tired to care whether he washes the dishes or not, then you can expect to see dirty dishes in the sink every morning.

Keeping an eye out for discipline issues can be a real pain, especially at the beginning of a female-dominant relationship. During this critical time, your man will want to make sure you are serious. He will repeatedly test your patience and see if you will follow through with punishing him. Call him out on your need to correct him, and make him promise to behave better in the future. He will eventually calm down enough for you to take one eye off him.

He's counting on you to enforce your authority. Without it, your orders are empty. So be stern. Be strict. Be unyielding. If you count down from three, be ready to do something truly terrifying at "one." Never back off without a good reason. Stand firm.

That said, there will be situations when it would be unreasonable to enforce your own rules. Life can get in the way of your best intentions. If your mother-in-law is visiting, your husband may not be able to serve you coffee naked. That's fine. The important thing is that you are the one who decides what is reasonable; it's not up to your partner's mood.

I find it useful to have a mental list of priorities that override my demands as a female dominant. If God, work, or family need my man's attention, he is excused from whatever I've asked him to do. If he would be required to do something illegal, immoral, or dangerous to complete one of my tasks, then he has the right to refuse and bring the conflict to my attention. My partner's life and well-being are in my hands, and it is my responsibility to make sure they are properly taken care of. Likewise, your partner trusts you enough to place himself in your hands.

~ Set Expectations ~

LOOK at your life. You can adjust it using your partner's help. What would you like to add or remove? Is there anything that he could do that would make your life easier? Is there anything he does to drive you crazy that you would like to correct?

Do you drink coffee every morning? He can make it for you. Does he leave his socks on the floor? He can start putting them in the laundry hamper. For that matter, he can take over your laundry duties altogether. He can also send you an email every afternoon at 3 PM, learn to drywall, save up for a trip to Europe, and take you out dancing at night. Anything you want.

Make a list of proposed changes with specific rules. Maybe your man will rub your feet while you watch TV in the evenings, refill your drinks at dinner, open your doors, and clear the kitchen before you go to bed. Talk with your partner to make sure your wishes are clear, with no practical objections. Then, take your list for a test drive: enforce it. (You will learn enforcement techniques soon.)

With a list in his hand and your eye on his performance, your partner will scramble to complete all of his duties. The submissive male wants to please you, so he will try to do his best. Of course, there will be lapses; your partner is only human, after all. As his dominant, you will deal with any issues as they arise. You can maintain the boundaries you have set by taking disciplinary measures and by tweaking your rules when it becomes absolutely necessary.

Remember to define what you want clearly. Your list of duties should be required, not optional. They may need to occur at a specific time or after a certain trigger. Figure out what is important to you in as specific a language as possible. (If your partner loves being micromanaged, you could even decree details right down to which color scrub brush he should use.)

You can always adjust, add to, and subtract from your list according to your needs. It will evolve as your relationship evolves, to meet your changing circumstances. If all goes well, the two of you will have some kind of list, written or unwritten, from now on.

~ Being Bossy ~

Being bossy means saying, "Darling, would you please...?"

Being bossy means saying, "Thank you so much for your help."

Being bossy means asking, "What is your objection?" and listening to the answer.

Of course, it can also mean saying, "On your knees, worm! Lick my boots!" and that sort of thing... but only if you so choose.

The point is, domination isn't required to be as bossy as you've been led to believe. You might be able to make verbal abuse work for an hour or two at a time, but it won't work in the context of a long-term relationship. If you want your "pathetic pig" to respect you, you must first respect him. (And since you're with him now, I'm sure you already do.)

No one can become a leader without first inspiring loyalty in their followers. Yes, a powerful bully might use armies and weapons to threaten a country – but those governments tend to topple as soon as the right back is turned. A cruel mistress may whip a man into scrubbing her floors, but he will likely cut corners and slack off in resentment as soon as she leaves the room.

A true leader will be someone worth obeying, someone who deserves to be followed. She can discipline others because she first disciplines herself. She demonstrates that she can be trusted to act with maturity.

A good leader doesn't bring others down. She lifts them up. She has faith that delays are temporary, that obstacles can be overcome, and that mistakes can be explained. She is reasonable, and will listen to similarly reasonable requests. She expects work to be done well because she always expects the best from her partner, and he is anxious to live up to her high opinion of him.

Men have a great deal of dignity – even men that fantasize about being degraded and abused. Deep down, they know their vulnerable efforts are not to be wasted on a tinpot dictator. They would rather bow to a queen. And to your man, that queen is you.

~ Giving Orders ~

IF you've ever had children or worked as any type of manager, you're probably used to giving orders. You got the hang of it quickly because you had to. You learned that if you want peace and quiet or that quarterly report, you need to let others know about it.

But if you're not used to being in authority, you might not be sure how to instruct others. You might expect your partner to be a mind reader, telling him to "Ow!" instead of "Get off my foot." You might be too politely vague to give him definite direction. You might rule with a limp fist by ending all of your statements with "Okay?"

If you want to be a convincing commander, then simply expect your partner to obey your every command. This isn't too far off the mark. He will never say no without good reason... and he'll be much more likely to follow your orders if you sound like you're not giving him any choice.

Most of your orders will be so small, you would think nothing of doing them yourself if someone asked: "Come here; turn off the light; wait a moment." Really, you've been telling your partner to do these things all along – but you likely phrased them as questions.

Many women fall into submissive habits without even realizing it. They unconsciously defer to their partner's tendencies. They ask "Is it okay if I..." and "Would you mind..." to be nice, without really thinking about it. They place their needs second in the household hierarchy – in money matters, in leisure time, in the bedroom – because it is easier than rocking the boat.

Even when trying out a "female dominant" relationship, a well-meaning woman may merely be following along with her partner's wishes. She will stifle her feelings of discomfort to humor him. She will act like she thinks a dominatrix is supposed to act – sternly stomping her foot and scolding – but she'll always wonder if she's doing it right. Is she faking it well enough to please her man? What would a *real* dominant woman do?

But there's no need to "fake it till you make it." Remember, your real dominance comes from being yourself. If you pursue what you want, you will naturally steer the ship. It doesn't matter if you want your man to weed the garden or learn ballet. It doesn't matter if you feel like wearing leather or lace or jeans. Seek your own happiness, and your man is bound to follow. He has no choice but to work with you. If you step outside of his boundaries, there's nothing he can do but pull up his stakes and scramble to catch up.

So don't fall into asking for endorsement. Don't check to make sure your needs are okay. Just go for it. State your desire. Request what you want, unapologetically. Discard that one little layer of hesitance and acknowledge your true feelings.

If you want something, say so. That's all it takes. No need to justify, defend, or apologize for it. Just tell your magic genie what you want – what you *really* want. Your wish is his command.

When you want to say...	*Try this instead:*
Can I ask you a favor?	Do me a favor and...
Would you like to go out?	Let's go out.
I wish we had more milk.	Buy a gallon of milk.
Let me know your schedule.	Send me your schedule.
Do you mind if I take this?	I'm taking this.
The car needs a wash.	Wash the car.
Is that okay with you?	Understood?

Do these examples sound blunt? Good! Remember, men are straightforward. They appreciate facts. What women want can be a mystery to them, but hard data is difficult to misinterpret.

If you're feeling thirsty, don't just tell your partner you're feeling thirsty. Tell him to bring you an iced tea. In a wine glass. With a slice of lemon. Whatever you want is yours – just as soon as you explain it.

Even with assertive phrasing, it's perfectly okay to say "please" and "thank you." Submissive men do not need to be threatened with challenges like "now" and "or else" to get things done. As far as they're concerned, those phrases are already implied.

For more on the language of leadership, check out business management books. They can introduce you to motivational techniques and tactful phrasing that will inspire your partner to excel at any task you assign him.

~ Reward and Punish ~

When your man does something pleasant that you'd like to see him repeat, praise him. When he does something unpleasant that you never want to see again, scold him. This is the simple truth behind training your submissive. Domination is not some complex and mysterious talent granted only to women in upper management. It's a straightforward method of behavior modification.

If your man does something wonderful, tell him why you are pleased and praise him for it. Oh, you love that he brought you flowers – it's so romantic and spontaneous, and you enjoy surprises! He remembered that your favorite is red roses, great! Explain all of this to him. Stroke his hair. Give him kisses. Most importantly, tell him he is a good boy. Praise his worth as a person.

If he disappoints you, don't belittle his worth. Just explain to him the behavior you expect from him, and how he failed to live up to it. Domination is not a license to criticize (unless you both like that sort of thing!). It is a practical program for improvement. Your corrections should be inspired by your faith in his ability to meet and even exceed your expectations. He is fine marble, yours to sculpt and polish to perfection. He will learn through your consequences.

Sometimes your partner will do something both good and bad, like send you a love poem full of typos. Explain why this is both good and bad, and give him both reward and punishment. He should not learn to pacify you with half-hearted efforts; you must encourage his best behavior, always.

So what do you do when he does something all bad?

Let's say he failed to mow the lawn like he said he would. There are two transgressions here: failure to complete a chore, and a broken promise. First, make sure he understands that these are not acceptable. Don't just let him agree; ask him to explain what he did wrong, and how he can improve in the future. Then, force him to amend his error.

He must correct his mistake. Send him to mow the lawn. It doesn't matter if the football game is on and the mower is out of gas – if he wants to be dominated, he can't skim out of it whenever he likes. He must complete your tasks. They are his responsibility, just as your responsibility is making sure he complies.

To further reduce the likelihood that he will disappoint you again, add an extra deterrent to the correction: punishment.

What your partner will consider punishment will vary by person. Some men hate spankings and some men love them. Some men hate doing chores and some men enjoy them. Some men will feel terrible taking a time-out in a corner, and some men will roll their eyes at how easy this is. Obviously, you want to select punishments that your partner dislikes, so as not to encourage more misbehavior. If you know your man well and listen to your instincts, you can select an appropriate deterrent.

Some of the punishments listed here may seem pretty shocking, even abusive. But you have no obligation to try any of them. You can find your own style of domestic discipline, doing whatever works for your relationship. If your man responds to a calm discussion of why you are disappointed, you may certainly stick to that – but it may become tedious for both of you rather quickly. The point here is not to punish your partner, but to encourage him to *avoid* punishment. If your first consequence is unpleasant enough, he will diligently try to avoid other transgressions in the future.

The worst punishment will always be removing yourself from his presence. He loves you and wants to be near you. Going away for a week without speaking to him is harsh treatment. Threatening to leave him altogether is pure abuse, and should be banned from your repertoire.

Whatever you choose, your punishment should be swift and fair. It is more effective to correct an error immediately after it happens and not a week later when you've both forgotten the details. Never punish while angry; take a step outside to think it over, if you must. Do not overreact. A misspoken word will warrant a laughing reprimand, not a strapping.

A note on physical punishment: I cannot fully comprehend why my partner needs this to feel complete, but I understand that he does. It gives him a sort of catharsis and a feeling of atonement for his sins. He feels better knowing his debt to me has been paid in full, and will not be held over his head with the manipulative emotional baggage that is so common in relationships. I do not enjoy having to punish him, but I know he appreciates it. I love him enough to be as strict as he needs.

The final step in the punishment process is forgiveness. Your expectations have been met and you both know he will try not to disappoint you again. Remember how beautiful he is for trying to please you, and grant him another chance.

Responding to good behavior:

- Show your delight
- Tell him why you are pleased
- Praise him
- Grant a reward (usually your words are enough!)

Examples of rewards:

- Praise ("Good boy! I'm proud of you. Great job!")
- Complimenting his work/skills/improvement
- Sex/orgasm
- His favorite fetish
- Petting, cuddling, kisses, time together
- A note explaining how happy you are to own him
- Additional privileges (a pillow for when he sleeps on the floor; allowing one more night out drinking)
- Demonstrations of your loving leadership, like a surprise date or a new toy you will both like
- Reminders of your ownership, like symbolic jewelry or sending him to work with a nice pink backside

Responding to bad behavior:

- Explain why you are disappointed
- Ask him to explain an understanding of his mistake
- Make him correct his error, if at all possible
- Punish him to deter future bad behavior
- Accept his atonement and forgive him

Examples of punishments:

- Scolding ("I am disappointed in you" is crushing)
- Corporal punishment/spanking (unless he likes it)
- Denial of sex/orgasm
- Writing page(s) of lines ("I will not talk in class, I will not talk in class…") or essays on virtue
- Standing in the corner/"time out"
- Dreaded chores (cleaning the oven/gutters)
- Kneeling on uncooked rice
- Exercise (such as push-ups, burpees, holding two buckets of water steady at shoulder height)
- Self-conscious humiliation (such as taking him out wearing your lip gloss/underwear, if he hates it)
- Grounding (no TV, internet, porn, beer…)
- Ironic punishments (such as a cold shower for forgetting to water your plants)
- Sleeping on the floor
- Lack of interaction with you
- Taking your ball home/"Pack up, we're leaving"
- Removal of a reward/privilege
- Ask him what he thinks would be an appropriate correction of his error, and adjust it to your taste

~ Answers and Objections ~

WHAT if he says no? This seems like an ominous possibility, right? But it's not very likely. In my years of domination, I don't think I've ever had a single power struggle staredown. All of the disagreements that came up were handled very smoothly. Even a momentary pause is usually enough to send my partner fumbling for an apology.

If your partner hesitates to follow an order, it's a simple matter to spur him into motion. Just prompt him to submit. Sometimes he forgets his role, and he will always attempt to please you if he can.

A sharp reminder will put things back in perspective. Here are a few good prompts to keep up your sleeve:

- "Boy!"
- "Are you complaining?"
- "Would you prefer to sleep on the floor tonight?"
- "Oh, you want to test out the new paddle?"
- "Do you know how many men would love to be in your position right now?"
- "I didn't ask for your opinion."
- "You don't get a vote."
- "What did I just say?!"
- "Now."

It's unlikely that your partner will object after he hears a statement like one of these. If he does, it means one of two things: a) he has a compelling concern that you should stop and listen to, or b) he is a "brat" who reflexively argues for the sake of argument, possibly angling for a punishment.

If it's the first case, be grateful. It's your partner's job to inform you of safety concerns, logistical difficulties, and so on, because they are important for you to hear. (Make sure you let him know this!) Allow him to air his objection for your consideration. Then you can decide if you need to back off, after all, or go ahead and press him through his recalcitrance. You're the boss, so the final call is your decision.

If it's the second case, and he's mouthing off to test you or goad you, then you can punish him to deter this behavior in the future. Since these fellows are often angling for something like a sexy spanking with a side of ear-burning scolding, make sure your actual punishment involves oven cleaning and tax forms.

Sometimes men will talk back because it's fun. You just dropped the perfect straight line and he couldn't let it pass by. You can tell when this is good-natured banter that wasn't meant to challenge you. Have a healthy laugh and banter back! If something doesn't feel right, though... well, ovens.

By the way, your partner may have a little repertoire of sayings up his sleeve for you, too, such as "Whatever my Mistress wants" and "As you say, Ma'am." Don't let him get away with these bland non-answers when you want to hear his real feelings. However, if you can train your own rote responses into him, such as "Yes, Ma'am, right away, Ma'am..." it will become pretty stimulating to hear your work. I recommend it.

~ It's Your Decision ~

A surprising number of men who think of themselves as "submissive" are more concerned with catering to their own needs than those of their partner. They think of female domination as a script, as costumes, as sexual positions. This type of man will coerce his wife into catering to a porn fantasy she is not the least bit interested in, as if she were merely his fetish vending machine.

It's unlikely that this man would buy the book you're reading now (at least, if he knew anything about it past the title). But I'm going to devote some time to him, because I suspect there's at least a tiny little bit of him in your partner.

I'm assuming your man came to you with a request to be more dominant. Now, he probably has a specific image in his head of what that looks like – a woman sitting on his face saying just the right things in just the right way. He thinks he'll never be completely happy in a relationship until this scenario happens.

The question is... do you want that woman to be you or someone else?

This is a serious question that deserves serious thought. Do you love your man enough to try this out with him, or do you trust your man enough to send him to a professional instead?

You can't just ignore his request and hope it goes away, because he'll never forget it. His fantasy will always eat at him. As his partner, you must make a choice: will you participate or not?

I can assure you that your partner found it terrifying to bring up the topic of female domination with you. He knew it could be a deal-breaker, that you might find it too strange, that you might leave him over it. He knows that it could be a deal-breaker for him, too, if you refuse him and he can only look forward to feeling unfulfilled for the rest of his life. Marriages can and do break up over this.

At the same time, he is wildly hopeful that you will love him enough to listen to his confidences, to help him out, to try new things with him. He trusts you with this most vulnerable side of him, and he prays you will take it as seriously as he does.

In some dumb, backward way, he thinks that if you try dressing up in latex for him and you like it too, the dilemma will be solved and you'll both live happily ever after.

But female dominance is so much more than dressing up. It is an amazing journey into vulnerability for both of you. You can be brave enough to be yourself unapologetically, and your partner can trust you enough to see him in very compromising positions. You can say, "This makes me uncomfortable," and he can say, "That makes me sad." Complete honesty with your romantic partner – can you imagine? Can you imagine what the sex will be like, five years from now, when you've lived through so many strange new adventures together and admitted how they really make you feel? Simply looking into each other's eyes will speak volumes.

Other couples go to their deathbeds never experiencing that level of closeness and intimacy. You have an incredible opportunity for more romance than you ever dreamed possible, and it's all because of your partner's strange request that you tie him up and spank him.

So if tying him up and spanking him sounds strange and disgusting to you, stand up straight and tell him so. Don't let him misbehave and whine and complain until you break down and do it for him. Say no! You're in charge. If you don't want to do it, don't do it. Have enough integrity to work out an option you can both live with.

If you learn one rule from this book, let it be this: *don't give in to pressure*. Your choices are your choices, and no one else's.

You have the right to refuse your partner's suggestions or actively choose to adopt them. Don't let him pressure you into reciting the script he's written in his head. Take the time to figure out what *you* want to do. Your long-term comfort, pleasure, and satisfaction is much more important to the relationship than appeasing him for one night.

This doesn't mean that you're rejecting your partner's wishes or that you're refusing to be his dominant. You *are* being dominant. That's how this works. You decide, and what you say goes. Your partner signed up for this ride, and you're the one steering. Of course you will factor your partner's happiness into your journey – it's entrusted to your care, after all. But the next destination is your call.

Someday, you might sit on his face in just the way that he likes. But it will be because you enjoy seeing what it does to him, and you love having that much control over him. It will be because you find it fun to play with him, not because he asked you to. And shouldn't playtime be fun?

Part IV

Scening

~ Of Scenes and Bedrooms ~

THIS book has been written for a woman learning to become more dominant in general. There's an alternate option: to act more dominant only for a short time, during a "scene." Scenes are what you generally see in pornography – an acting session of flogging, or "forced" crossdressing, or slavery in chains. Commands are strict and fierce. The scene can include overt acts of sexuality or subtle undercurrents of sensuality.

I'll be honest: there's no practical need for me to include this section in the book. A dominant woman can control her man without a single evening of kinky sex. But sexual desire is the number one thing that will get a man's attention. You can use this knowledge to your advantage, if you are so inclined.

No one expects you to "put out." As a dominant woman, you are in control in the bedroom. You can refuse sex altogether, or demand it how and when you like. If you find kinky sexual scenarios as intriguing as your man does, then you can choose to add them into your relationship. Scenes can be a very rewarding and intoxicating spice.

The scene requires more intensely concentrated effort and planning than the slow simmer of a female-led relationship. It is an experiment in sexuality. How hot can a spanking be for both of you? How will your partner react if you do this or that? How far will he go to please you?

A scene is a formal event with several steps:

First is the negotiation, a conversation to responsibly plan your scene. You and your partner discuss which fetish you would like to explore, limits that cannot be broken, safety concerns, hopes and fears, and so on. With this knowledge, you can dream up a fantasy scene to surprise your partner with. If you were making a set for a movie, what props would you use? What would the script be about? You will find yourself mulling over your options in your private time until you have a pretty good idea of what you want to happen. (If you spend your *very* private time thinking on this topic, you will be inspired with especially sexy twists.)

Next comes the psychological build-up. You set a date and time for the scene. You may send your man flirtatious notes during the day to remind him of what's coming up. He may prepare by grooming himself, wearing special clothing for you, and/or picking up supplies. You will naturally continue to daydream and refine your fantasy in anticipation of his visit. Prep your props and dress for your scene.

There should be a clear signal when the scene begins that both partners are stepping into their roles. You may tell him to kneel at your feet or strip to his underwear. You may lock a collar onto his neck or make him recite a ritual greeting. Whatever you do, you will quickly and firmly establish that you're in charge and your man is expected to follow your orders.

The bulk of the scene is an exploration of the planned fetish. This may start with a script, but it's easier to let the scene unfold naturally. Using the skills you learned in the *Confidence* chapters, you give your man a task, such as dressing as a maid and cleaning the house. You appraise his job using the skills you learned in the *Training* chapters. If your maid does a bad job, it would make sense to punish him with a spanking, and so on.

This sounds vague, and it is. There is no way to plan for every possible variation on female domination. Only one rule always holds true: you are in charge, so both of you will follow the thread of whatever you say. If you want him to clean the house, you're in for a cleaning fantasy. If you want him to make love to you, you're going to have one very attentive lover for the night.

This isn't a final exam. It's playtime. So don't take it too seriously. You're allowed to make mistakes. The goal is your amusement. If you're giggling, you're doing great.

Listen to your instincts until you are satisfied that the scene is at a good stopping point (or that the mood is going downhill and it's time to call it quits). Cuddling in the afterglow is usually a good stopping point!

After a scene, give your partner a chance to recuperate during "aftercare." Help him rehydrate with water and refuel with a snack. Apply ice or ointment if the scene was physically demanding. Stay with your partner until he relaxes enough to want to talk about it. Then discuss what happened.

Your post-scene discussion will help you understand what works for both of you and what doesn't. It will help you avoid pitfalls in the next scene and identify new fetishes you can explore. Best of all, it will give you a chance to know your partner better. The two of you will grow emotionally closer, one scene at a time.

Creating a scene:

- Negotiate to select a fetish and address concerns
- Dream up what the scene will look like
- Refine the details in your "private" time
- Build suspense and prep the stage
- Launch the scene with your opening line
- Explore your planned fetish
- Listen to your instincts for what to do next
- Wrap up the scene at a good stopping point
- Provide aftercare
- Have an intimate talk with your partner

Some possible opening lines:

- "Boy, kneel at my feet. Kiss them."
- "On all fours. Crawl! Follow me."
- "Strip to your skin. Fold those clothes neatly!"
- "Bend your neck for your collar."
- "Tell me who owns you. Louder! Good…"
- "Raise your arms and turn slowly for inspection."
- "Lower your eyes and shut your mouth. You will not speak until I give you permission. Nod yes."
- "You're late. You know what happens when you keep me waiting. Get the paddle. Now!"
- "There is a toy on the bed. Fetch it here."
- "I plan to inspect your last task. Show it to me."

~ Games to Start Out With ~

"Where do I start? What can I do?" the newbie mistress often asks. The answer she tends to hear is unenlightening: "Do whatever you like."

Now, while this is perfectly true, it's pretty impractical to work with. So, here are some examples of fun, easy games to try out as a new female dominant. You can use them in formal scenes or just to amuse yourself this evening. You can try one idea at a time or combine a few at once. You can edit the details to your tastes. You can do whatever you like, you see!

As you gain more experience at domination, you will discover the dynamics that you most enjoy, and you will dream up more and more engaging entertainment for yourself and your partner.

Some possible games:

· You will relax in one spot – say, a bubble bath – while he waits to fetch anything and everything you need.
· He will act as your shopping chauffeur for the evening: driving, carrying packages, and opening doors. He is not allowed to critique your purchases.
· He is not allowed to touch you anywhere except where you tell him to. (How about a nice foot rub? Then maybe a back rub...)
· He will memorize and recite a nursery rhyme for your amusement. He must perform in a funny pose.

· He must cook dinner for you alone, serve the meal, and clean up in respectful silence, speaking only when spoken to. (Bonus points for remembering your favorite meal.)
· When he makes a mistake, he must add a token to a demerit jar – to be paid in full at the end of the night.
· He is not allowed to raise his head above yours.
· He must make sure your glass is never empty.
· He will be tied to the bedposts while you toy with his helplessness. He is not allowed to beg.
· He must ask permission to leave the room.
· He must stop mid-sentence and kneel whenever you tell him to.
· You'll only use formal titles all night: boy/slave/pet for him, Mistress/Ma'am/Milady for you (or whatever turns you both on the most).
· He is required to use your formal title at the end of every sentence.
· Tell him to complete the three chores you've been hinting he should do. If he gets all three right, he'll get a reward....
· He is only allowed to answer "yes" to any question you ask that night. (Ha, ha!)

Mistakes will be handled in whatever way you feel is most appropriate to the moment – a playful spank for a slip of the tongue, or a stern correction for a real misdeed. Be consistent, and be ready to live with your own consequences. After all, you can only enforce as many rules as you can remember.

Trust your instincts. You will get to know them well.

~ Safewords ~

If your partner has a certain fetish that sounds non-consensual on the surface, he may want to establish a safeword. A safeword is a signal to stop, as opposed to objections that might just be playful acting.

So, while your man lives out his fantasy of forced submission, he might say, "No, no, I don't want to, please don't make me," and really mean "I do want to, please make me!" To avoid confusion, the two of you can pre-arrange a specific word that means "I really, seriously, honestly do want to stop," like "mercy" or "pineapple." Now, no matter how much your partner protests, you can continue to play with him until you hear these phrases.

One common set of safewords is "Red," "Yellow," "Green." *Red* means stop; *yellow* means slow down, or continue more gently; *green* means all is well, go ahead. You can use them as prompts: "Are you calling yellow? Is that a red?"

In practice, I rarely hear my partner use a safeword, because I rarely do this kind of roleplaying. If he tells me he's feeling "the bad kind of pain," you can be sure I'll stop everything to make sure he's okay. So, no matter what safewords you've established, don't grow complacent. Be responsible and keep your ears open for problems.

~ Stop and Think About It ~

Before your first scene, you may be afraid that something will come up that you won't know how to handle. Your man will throw you a curveball, and unlike the sassy dominatrix in all the videos, you won't know what to say. Well, something might come out of your mouth, but you're sure it won't be anything witty, clever, or hot. It might even be, "Umm..."

This is fine. We are lovers, not paid actors. Your response to your partner should be natural and heartfelt. If you can't say something natural and heartfelt, don't force it.

Your man is not a mind reader. He has no idea what is going on in your head. He doesn't know that you feel uncertain, or that you aren't sure what to do next. He's not critiquing your performance. He just knows that his job is to pay attention to the next word out of your mouth.

There is nothing wrong with admitting that you need more time. The phrase "I'll think about it," always puts you in control. Asking him to explain himself works just fine. If you need more information, request it. If you don't want to be pressured into a decision, say so. A demand to be quiet while you think can actually be extremely sexy.

And on a practical note, I've noticed that a rummage through the toy bag when I am unsure of my next step always gives me surprisingly good ideas.

~ Take Your Time ~

One of the first dominant things I ever did was pressure a friend for a proper neck rub. I had a tension headache that was interfering with my work, and pain medicine hadn't put a dent in it. Since this was a recurring condition, the friend in question had given me neck rubs before. Every time, he would sigh and grumble that his fingers were tired, his hands hurt, and so on. But he was my only option. When I needed pain relief, I generally took what I could get from him and let him get on with his day.

So he was rubbing my shoulders (not yet sighing in boredom), and I was nearing the point of politeness. I knew his complaints would start coming at any moment. I felt 70% better. That was good enough, wasn't it? I could thank him and leave before I annoyed him, and it would be easier for everyone. Wouldn't it?

Except that my neck would still hurt. Why should I continue to suffer, just for the sake of someone else's feelings? Weren't my feelings just as valuable as his? I forced myself to stay put, talking myself out of fleeing.

He rubbed to 80%. He shook out his fingers as if they felt fatigued. Again I felt the urge to preempt his complaints by getting up to leave, but I stopped myself.

I did thank him, though. He took it as a signal to quit. Screwing up my courage, I explained that I hadn't wanted him to quit. He started massaging again.

He rubbed to 90% and then he stopped. Did he gripe at me? Did he tell me that I was selfish to need a neck rub? No. He didn't think there was anything wrong with me or my request. He just asked, "Can I take a break for a second?"

I gave him permission.

In the end, he gave me a massage that cured my headache. All I had to do was wait... and allow myself to feel worth it.

You are worth it. Don't let yourself be rushed. Don't roll over so your man's needs can override yours. You matter. You're being pampered. You may not be used to it, but you can learn to accept it and enjoy it.

Whether you're getting a back rub or enjoying a decadent session of cunnilingus, your man wants to be there, putting in that effort. He's pampering you for the sake of your pleasure. That's what makes him happy.

So don't feel guilty. This is *your* scene. Take your time and enjoy yourself for as long as you like. Your man will love you for it.

~ Caring Too Much ~

When I sent my first fledgling dominant out into the world to try her hand at my tricks of the trade, she came back with fidgety fingers and an uncertain shuffle of one foot. "Well," she said, not quite meeting my eye, "I, uh... kept wondering if my partner was enjoying himself. Is that okay?"

Yes, it's okay. We have this idea that dominant women are somehow heartless and selfish, cruelly beating innocent and miserable male victims – when, really, it's usually the innocent men requesting our abuse. Women are generally pretty accommodating and friendly creatures, so if we're open-minded enough, we're willing to help our guy live out his fantasies.

(Oddly, I've heard this problem from the male end, too: "Is it okay that I liked it?" You poor confused fellows!)

My dear reader, there's no need to act sadistic to be the one on top. There is a difference between cruelty and control. Look at it this way: When you go to the dentist, you pay to put a professional in charge of your body, trusting him to choose what's best for your health. You want him to be in control; you don't want him to be a sadist!

Some couples like to make a show of sadism because it underscores a feeling of imbalance of power, and they find that arousing. Or, at least one of the participants finds some pain erotic. That's all it is: a consensual turn-on. Pain for the sake of pain is not a requirement for a female-dominated relationship. If it works for you and your partner, that's fine.

There is absolutely nothing wrong with being loving and nurturing and listening to your partner's needs. In my opinion, a good dominant will always want to be that responsible.

Responsibility is sexy. Own it. Use it. Have a good idea of what your partner's boundaries are, what he's afraid of, and what he wants. Protect your "property" with all your heart, even as you push him to go further. As long as you respect his mental health and physical safety, there are no limits to what the two of you can explore. Sadistic, or not.

Female dominance fantasies are supposed to be fun. If he's not having fun, then chances are, you aren't having fun either. And the feeling is mutual! The trick is to find something that you both enjoy.

No one gets it right on the first try. Experiment. Test out ideas you find intriguing. Eventually, something will hit your sweet spot. Right on!

~ Fetishes ~

It's all very well to say "experiment" and "try things out" when you don't know what's available to try. There are so many interesting variations on female domination out there that I could never hope to work through them all. (Nor would I want to try everything I've seen!)

You might be saying, "I don't even know what I'm interested in yet!" I suggest exploring a pornography website to see what lifts your eyebrows. After you browse for a few minutes, what keywords do you start searching for? Which images haunt you, days later? What do you think of when you masturbate?

Just because you find something sexually interesting doesn't give it any profound meaning. You might like it one week and be tired of it the next. It might be more exciting in your head than it is in person. It might be something you like, but your partner doesn't. You might grow gradually more attracted to an idea over time. It's all good. Just take your time and enjoy discovering more and more about yourself.

Here are a few general categories of fetishes that could be interesting starting points for you:

· *Bondage* – You tie your man to the bedposts, spread eagle; you chain him to the sink until the dishes are done; you roll his lower body up in a blanket or plastic wrap, mummifying him...

· *Chivalry* – Your man acts like a gentleman, opening your doors, carrying your bags, and paying for your dinner...
· *Crossdressing* – You force your man to secretly wear panties to work; you show him how to put on your makeup; you make him clean the house in a French maid outfit...
· *Foot worship* – Your man gives you pedicures and foot rubs; you tease him with sexy footwear or caresses with your feet; he kisses and licks your toes...
· *Human furniture* – Your man holds your dinner tray, acts as your bath towel rack, or curls up under your feet as your footstool...
· *Humiliation/degradation* – You tell him to sing a silly song, bark like a dog, or beg, and laugh at his discomfort; you call him unflattering names, as in "Do it now, bitch!"; you walk him like a dog... (Don't do these in public; respect the mental rights of others.)
· *Roleplaying* – The two of you pretend to be nurse and patient, schoolteacher and student, or policewoman and suspect...
· *Sadomasochism* – You give your partner painful but non-injurious stimulation that he enjoys, such as spanking, biting, or pinching; you carefully release his endorphins using toys such as nipple clamps or crops... (Educate yourself, through research and instruction, on how to do these things safely.)
· *Sensation play* – You blindfold him and tease him with feathers, silk, ice, tickling, clothespins, and other mysterious torments...

- *Service-oriented slavery* – Your man cooks your meals, does your chores, and refills your drinks...
- *Spanking* – You take him over your knee for "funishment" or disciplinary punishment; he stands or bends over and you turn his buttocks red with a flogger or crop...
- *Tease and denial* – You tie up and touch him until he begs; you withhold sex as motivation; you reach orgasm but you refuse to let your partner finish... (Yes, some men really do enjoy this!)
- *Verbal training* – You teach him to say "Yes, Mistress, thank you, Mistress" and "Thank you, Ma'am, may I have another..."

If you're ready to get to know your partner more intimately than you've ever imagined, then compare your reactions to this list of scenarios. Each of you can write out the ideas you find even a little bit intriguing, then sit down together to share your notes. If you are lucky, your interests may intersect closely enough to experiment.

Your partner might like the idea of something you personally find baffling – but if you are willing to ask a few compassionate questions, he can help you understand where he is coming from. Likewise, he will learn how to meet you where you're at. He might even be able to find insight from your interests and point you in a direction not listed here.

Be bold and give communication a shot. You will understand each other better than ever.

~ Putting It All Into Practice ~

What does it mean to be a dominant woman in charge of a submissive man?

If you've gotten this far, you've learned that it isn't as disturbing as society seems to think. It's a mutually rewarding relationship full of care and respect.

Your partner has a romantic desire to please you, no matter what. In time, you will understand how taking charge of him makes him feel safe, appreciated, and aroused. You will discover that it makes you feel loved, rewarded, and self-possessed.

The two of you can talk about anything together. Share your new understanding; communicate your thoughts and fears. You can fix any problem. You can get to know each other deeply and intimately by facing new and exciting challenges side by side.

If you haven't already, give your partner a list of things to do – your new requirements for your relationship. Take him in hand. Enforce his duties with consequences. Give him the tough love he craves and see how pleasantly you are rewarded.

If you are curious about his fetishes, then plan a night to try them out. Don't feel pressured to perform. There is no wrong way to play. Take your time, experiment, and discover what you enjoy.

As you gain more experience, things will get easier, and sexier, and stricter. You'll learn to press your advantage; you'll learn that he likes giving up more and more control to you. He can stop at any time – but he won't want to.

No matter what the two of you do, open communication is essential. Get regular updates on how your partner feels. Make sure he understands your concerns and needs. A female-led relationship should never involve resentment – for either partner. You are a team, a symbiosis, capable of making each other happier than you've ever dreamed.

~ New Beginnings ~

My compliments, my dear reader. You were curious enough to make it through the whole book – an introduction to a strange new land, if there ever was one.

The woman who opened the first page is gone. In her place is someone who sees a wider world of opportunity spread out before her.

This woman is incredibly lucky, because she has a man with a unique need to please her. She knows that if she listens to her instincts deeply enough, if she learns to trust them, she will find an inner confidence to ask for whatever she wants.

And she knows there's no reason to be hesitant about it any longer.

~ THE VIEW FROM THE BOTTOM ~
A Submissive's Addendum

As I read through this book, I saw the truth in it. The benefits to the woman in the dominant/submissive relationship were evident. But you might ask yourself, what of the man? What goes through the mind of the submissive man? Even that term is a misnomer. I am not a "submissive man." I am a man who chooses to submit, and to a very special person in particular. Your man is likely the same way. Just as a knight would not pledge their allegiance to anyone, just like the knight would not serve any random person that calls upon him, so too does the "submissive man" choose who to submit to. And in your case, he's chosen you. Congratulations.

As has been pointed out, there are many reasons why a man might choose to submit to you. They are as varied as the men themselves. What I want to point out, though, is what makes this submission thing so alluring. What makes me want to scrub my beloved's floors so that she does not have to?

The first allure is her confidence. Most men are attracted to confidence. To a man that is strong enough to be submissive, that confidence in a woman is intoxicating. It is a heady aphrodisiac indeed. To a man that is insecure in himself, the confidence of a woman is intimidating. That man might avoid it, or lash out at it by insults and jokes. Such a man does not merit the attention of the confident woman. The truly secure man will find your confidence irresistible. In this way, you'll be able to tell who is worthy of you.

The second allure of submission is direction. Many "submissive men" have high-stress jobs, and are otherwise in charge of every aspect of their lives. I know that after an entire day of calling the shots, of solving everyone's problems, of analyzing and negotiating solutions, it is a relief to simply be told what to do. Do this, do that. Sit here, rub my feet. It is a balm for the busy mind. Though it might appear that the exchange is one-sided, I assure you, ladies, the man is enjoying it and receiving just as much in return.

The third allure is fulfillment of a man's instinct. Men have a biological need to protect, to provide. Being a doting attendant merely amplifies this need and directs it in productive ways. Gone are the days when I'd have to bring down a wildebeest to provide food. Instead, I can provide a nice, romantic dinner. Is this submissive? Perhaps. Would a woman like this arrangement? Undoubtedly. Does the man feel fulfilled by getting praise for a meal well-served? Of course.

The fourth allure is the exercise of chivalry. To the man that is so disposed, serving is an expression of love. I do not scrub the floors because I love scrubbing floors. I scrub the floors because I love the thought of my beloved not having to do so. I don't wash her car because I like washing cars (I do, actually, a little). I do so because I think of the satisfaction she will feel when she sits in it. There are a hundred little ways of serving, from opening doors to fetching a glass of water. Each little thing is an exercise of chivalry which, sadly, is sorely lacking in our society.

There are other aspects of the female-led relationship that are alluring – too many to go into here. Rest assured, ladies, that the man who seeks out such a relationship will be happy in seeing you pleased and satisfied, however deeply you choose to claim your power.

~ About the Author ~

Ms. Dvanna Hightower spends her days as a modest entrepreneur and her nights as immodestly as possible. With a glass of Cabernet in one hand and a man under one heel, she pens smoldering erotica laced with playful creativity. She has sampled various flavors of kink since the first blush of the internet. She loves science fiction, absurdist humor, and devoted pets (especially the human kind).

~ Dawn of Chastity ~
Dvanna Hightower

WHAT goes through the mind of a female dominant? Ms. Hightower offers a candid peek into her bedroom, sharing the most intimate details of a steamy morning encounter with her beloved male slave.

Kept locked in chastity for weeks at a time, her desperate partner will do anything to please her – and she knows it. He has been trained to attend to her every need. He offers her coffee, devotion, and sexual service. Knowing well his weaknesses, she takes advantage of them... and him.

Written with honesty and immediacy, this short diary entry will give you insight into life between two lovers descending deep into each other's minds... and the aroused delight a woman feels when truly pleased by the service of her boy.

~ THE LADY'S WILL ~
Raquel Rivers

WHEN eccentric Victoria Lancaster passes away, she leaves her niece Adele in charge of her Welsh estate. Demure Adele is suddenly thrust into a world more opulent than she ever imagined – one of servile attendants and pampered luxury. As she uncovers her aunt's secret life, Adele finds her sexual power awakening and the men around her falling at her feet... except the one she wants most.

Is Adele strong enough to tame the man she desires? Might her aunt's mysterious past help her? Follow Adele's steamy journey from shy librarian to mistress of the house as she abides by the lady's will.

Printed in Germany
by Amazon Distribution
GmbH, Leipzig